CHESTERFIELD TRAMWAYS

Series editor Robert J Harley
Barry M. Marsden

MP Middleton Press

Front Cover: Horse Car 7 meets Electric Car 9 on the loop outside the new tram depot on the 3rd of December 1904, during the latter's first test trials along the Brampton section of the line. The blue of the cover of this book is similar to the main panels of the horse car. The brown is close to the lower panels of the electric tram.

Published July 2004

ISBN 1 904474 37 3

Design   *Deborah Esher*
                 David Pede

Published by
                 Middleton Press
                 Easebourne Lane
                 Midhurst, West Sussex
                 GU29 9AZ
Tel: 01730 813169
Fax: 01730 812601
Email: info@middletonpress.co.uk
www.middletonpress.co.uk

Printed & bound by MPG Books Ltd, Bodmin, Cornwall

CONTENTS

Brampton Terminus	1	High Street	68	Sheffield Road	93
Tram Depot	26	Burlington Street	70	Dark Lane	102
West Bars	46	Cavendish Street	78	Whittington Terminus	107
New Square	52	Holywell Cross	88	End of an Era	118
Low Pavement	58	Holywell Street	90	Finale	120

INTRODUCTION AND ACKNOWLEDGEMENTS

I was born and brought up in Chesterfield, and lived for many years opposite the Thornfield Depot of the Corporation Transport Department which replaced the old tram depot on Chatsworth Road in 1927 after the changeover from trams to trolleybuses. I was a student in Sheffield in 1960 when the city terminated its first tram era, and was lecturing in Bradford in 1974 when its trolleybuses were withdrawn – the last to run in Britain. These events must have stimulated my interest in electric transport, and I have studied and written about the trams and trackless of my native town over many years. This book is a pictorial journey, as detailed histories of the undertaking can be consulted in the appropriate publications.

I trust the contents of this work will interest all students of horse and electric transport in England, and will evoke nostalgic memories of a much different world, and may stimulate the decreasing few who remember the days when these vehicles glided along the thoroughfares of the town. The electric tramway system in Chesterfield was planned as a reversed letter 'L', and the journey begins at the western extremity at Brampton Terminus where the Terminus Hotel stood for some 96 years before its untimely demolition in 2002. The route proceeds eastwards through the town centre, then extends northwards as far as the other terminus at Whittington Moor.

The photographs which illustrate the ride come from a variety of sources, many originating as commercial postcards, though a number of individual pictures are also present. The main contributions come via the collections of Alan Bower, Chesterfield Local Studies Library, Chesterfield Borough, my own assemblage, and that of the now defunct Chesterfield Transport Department. Where the source is known the photograph is duly credited, but the origins of some are obscure to say the least, and any inadvertent omissions in the acknowledgements are regretted. Thanks are due to Glynn Waite for pictures of the Chesterfield tickets from his extensive collection.

I have researched the history of Chesterfield tramways over many years, and one real pleasure was in seeing the restoration of Chesterfield Car 7 at Crich which was resurrected from the remains of the conveyance which served as a holiday home at Two Dales for many decades. One Red Letter Day was the 11th October 1999 when by kind courtesy of John Shawcross I was permitted to drive the car along the length of the track at Crich, the memory of which will last as long as I live.

GEOGRAPHICAL SETTING

Dominated by the justly famed 'Crooked Spire' of the Church of St Mary and All Saints, the ancient borough of Chesterfield, founded by the Romans as a fort and settlement around AD55 – 'the field of the camp or fort' - sits on a low hill above the confluence of the rivers Hipper and Rother. It is located on the Coal Measures at the centre of the once prolific Yorkshire, Nottinghamshire and Derbyshire coalfield, and coal mining was once the principal occupation of its male workforce. Its once proud boast was that it occupied a place as 'the Centre of Industrial England.' To the west of the town lie the hills and dales of the picturesque Peak District National Park.

At the time of the trams no less than three railways ran through the town, serving three separate stations and providing an excellent communications network. Chesterfield was the first English town to use electricity to illuminate its streets, in 1881, and in the early 1900s was home to a number of flourishing iron and steel works, potteries and factories producing cardboard and surgical dressings. In 1901 its population was 27,000, which by 1921 had more than doubled.

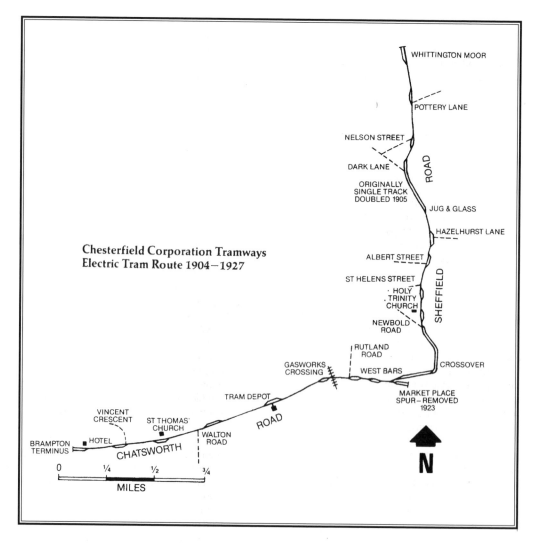

WHITTINGTON MOOR

POTTERY LANE

NELSON STREET

DARK LANE

ROAD

ORIGINALLY
SINGLE TRACK
DOUBLED 1905

JUG & GLASS

HAZELHURST LANE

Chesterfield Corporation Tramways
Electric Tram Route 1904–1927

ALBERT STREET

ST HELENS STREET

SHEFFIELD

HOLY
TRINITY
CHURCH

NEWBOLD
ROAD

RUTLAND
ROAD

GASWORKS
CROSSING

WEST BARS

CROSSOVER

TRAM DEPOT

MARKET PLACE
SPUR – REMOVED
1923

VINCENT
CRESCENT

ST THOMAS'
CHURCH

ROAD

N

BRAMPTON
TERMINUS

HOTEL

WALTON
ROAD

CHATSWORTH

0   ¼   ½   ¾

MILES

HISTORICAL BACKGROUND

The Chesterfield and District Tramways Company came into being in 1879 to provide the town's first transport service, though it did not commence operations until November 1882. Despite a number of proposed lines, the only length of track ever completed was a 1¼ mile/2km stretch of standard gauge track from Low Pavement in the town centre westwards as far as Walton Lane, Brampton. The company operated three trams. Cars 1 and 2 were Eade's reversible double-deckers, whilst Car 3 was a 16 seat single-decker. The company never achieved any measure of solvency, operating on a shoestring basis for less than three years which were marked only by general unreliability and poor timekeeping. It was no surprise when it went into liquidation with debts of £500.

A new body, the Chesterfield Tramways Company, took over in December 1886 and in 1890 they increased the car fleet by the purchase of two more single-deckers, Cars 4 and 5. In 1897 Chesterfield Corporation, following the general trend of municipal tramway ownership, purchased the undertaking by offering the company generous terms which they gratefully accepted. Following the takeover in November, they bought another single-decker, No.6, and reduced overall fares from 2d to Id. Two further single-deckers, Nos.7 and 8, joined the fleet, and the facility flourished. Horse car 8 was preserved as a summerhouse when electric traction commenced. It was fully restored in the 1980s and is now a permanent exhibit at Crich.

In 1903 the corporation sought to augment their horse car fleet by buying a redundant double-decker from Sheffield at the knockdown price of £5, though a year earlier there were reports that the tramtrack was worn out, and in need of relaying. It was decided that the line should be both extended westward and northward to the existing borough boundaries and electrified. A newly-formed Electric Tramways Committee put forward a parliamentary bill to that effect. In the Summer of 1904 work commenced on laying the new track and stringing the overhead wire. The line, mostly single track with turnouts, but doubled through the narrow town-centre streets, was completed by late November. Due to weekend congestion the facility was operated as two separate sections on Saturdays with termini at Low Pavement and Cavendish Street, where a facing crossover allowed two cars to park side-by-side.

The new line was 3⅝ miles/5.8km long, with the running wire carried on a mixture of side-arm poles and twin poles with span wires. The rolling stock consisted initially of 12 Brush-built open-toppers of the 'Aston' type, seating 22 passengers in the lower saloon, and 34 on the top deck. Painted in carmine red and primrose, the vehicles were of a standard pattern, with direct staircases, but boasted state-of-the-art Brush Radial trucks of an 8ft 6in/2590mm wheelbase as against the usual 6ft/1828mm. These promised a steadier ride, and some flexibility on curves. Each tram was 26ft/7924mm long and was powered by two 25hp Westinghouse motors. There was no opening ceremony, and the line was opened in stages from the 20th December 1904 till the end of January 1905, with the through fare set at 3d.

The facility enjoyed an encouraging first few years of operation thou gh running costs always kept pace with revenue. In 1907 two further trams, Nos. 12 and 13 joined the rolling stock, though these vehicles ran on Brush Flexible Axle trucks, also of an 8ft 6in wheelbase. In 1909, Brush built a water car, No. 15, designed to the specification of Robert Acland, the Tramways Manager. By 1909 faults were becoming apparent in the single line and loop system, evidenced by heavy wear on the curves and at loop points. In the years before World War I receipts failed to improve

and the tramway was caught in the general trap caused by building loans which had been spread over too long a period. Tramways which had operated on bare profits began to encounter increasing deficits as their components aged.

In 1914 three new Brush cars, Nos. 16-18, joined the fleet, the first to be fitted with top-covers, and running on Peckham P22 Pendulum trucks of an 8ft/2400mm wheelbase. The war caused further complications to the undertaking, with shortages of manpower and materials, and this was exacerbated by a severe fire which gutted the tramshed in October 1916, and badly damaged several vehicles. Car 17 was burned out and completely rebuilt, whilst Car 7 was restored with a top-cover. By 1919 Cars 6,8,11 and 12 had also been retrospectively top-covered.

By 1920 the condition of the trams, track and overhead were giving cause for serious concern, and the corporation's transport expansion was becoming concentrated on the motorbus side of the enterprise. The track and trams were kept serviceable by patching-up exercises, but by 1924 the Tramways Committee had determined on trolleybus replacement. This took place in 1927, when the overhead was converted in two stages. The Market Place-Brampton line was first adapted to railless operation, motorbuses taking over from the trams, which however still served the Cavendish Street-Whittington Moor section, though operating with top-covered cars only.

On 23rd May 1927, Car 14, suitably bedecked with flags and bunting, undertook the final run from Cavendish Street to Whittington, carrying local councillors and other dignitaries. The car returned to the depot, and the new service, spearheaded by 14 single-deck Straker-Clough trolleybuses, commenced operations that same day. It was a new era, but the trackless service lasted only a bare 11 years, less than half that of the tramcars.

When the trams were abandoned, the bodies were disposed of locally. Car 7 found its way to Two Dales where it served as a holiday cottage for many years. In 1973 the semi-derelict property was purchased by the Tramway Museum Society (TMS) at Crich, and was selected by the Tramcar Sponsorship Organisation (TSO) for restoration. This was carried out at Crich between 1993-6 at a cost of £120,000. This vehicle, in immaculate condition, now runs regularly at the museum and is a testament to the work of the TMS and the TSO.

BRAMPTON TERMINUS

1.   Early tickets which include, on the left, F5007, issued on the horse cars when the corporation took over the undertaking in 1897. Its survival is something of a miracle as passengers were told to destroy them after leaving the car. On the right D-0000 was the first ever ticket issued on the electric cars for a first day journey on 20th December 1904 from Low Pavement to Brampton terminus.

2.   Brand-new Car 9 is shown at Brampton on the first trial with Tramway Manager, Robert Acland, manning the controls, with his wife and child on his left. Behind the apprehensive-looking cyclist is the Old Pheasant Inn, soon scheduled for demolition to make way for the aptly named Terminus public house.

3.   Motorman Marshall poses with his conductor on Car 7, the most photographed vehicle in the whole fleet, at the terminus during the first winter of electric tram operation on the left-hand line of the twin track. Note the sylvan setting and the appalling state of the road margins.

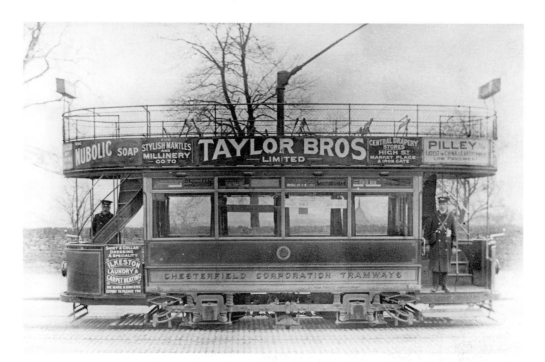

4.   A splendid side view of one of the new cars at Brampton reveals the details of the 8ft 6in/2.6metres radial truck and the electric track brake. The window bill, detailing that 'The Ladder of Life' was showing at the Chesterfield Theatre Royal, neatly dates the photograph to February 1905.

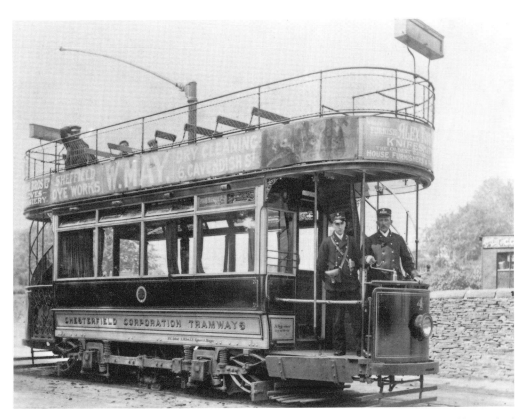

5.   Car 4 is at Brampton. This shot shows the kepi-style caps which replaced the earlier peaked ones. The picture shows the patent brass bar above the platform step. Raising it lowered the step, whilst lowering it to the horizontal folded it in the position shown. The day is windy, judging by the upper deck passenger who is holding firmly on to his hat! The motorman is Cyril Hopkinson, the conductor Derward Lowe.

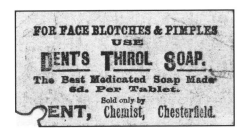

6.   Car 7 again and another pre-1906 view has Driver Stone at the controls and the Old Pheasant Inn still standing behind the vehicle. Note the rope to the right of the crew for swinging the trolleyboom at the termini. A proud father holds his baby for the benefit of the camera.

——————▶

7.   The Terminus Inn is shown nearing completion during 1906, a useful watering hole for passengers frozen on the upper decks of tramcars on cold journeys from town. The twin tracks can be seen in their bed of stone setts, as can the twin poles and span wire which carried the overhead all the way to the Market Place.

——————▶

8.   96 years later and the forlorn-looking inn awaits its fate, demolition at the hands of the council. Note the pub sign, which usually depicted vehicles which bore little resemblance to cars which actually plied the route. The one shown here actually boasts a blue livery! The premises were razed in mid-2002.

9.   Car 4 waits on the left-hand line at Brampton, just behind the track terminations seen to the left of the lady cyclist. In this photograph the Terminus Inn has replaced its predecessor. Note the time clock on the right-hand traction pole.

10.   The inevitable Car 7 poses at Brampton around 1910 with Motorman Bennett on the front platform. He began as a youthful conductor, and eventually became an inspector prior to his untimely death at the age of 37. The conductor is C.L. Marsden, though no relative as far as I am aware.

11. Car 12 is shown post World War I with its new top-cover and mixed crew. The corporation logo on the rocker panel is in a non-standard small lettering style. The destination boxes had by this time been removed in favour of boards carried in the lower side windows. The motorman is Jack Gretton, the conductress Elizabeth Kneale.

12.   Car 6, also by now top-covered, is depicted at the same venue. Note the weathered upperworks and sagging platforms that bespeak hard usage. On this tram the neat early gold lettering has been replaced by large black characters. The driver is John Rouse, the conductor Gary Gascoyne.

13.   Another careworn car was No.4, here posed post-war in the still picturesque surroundings of the terminus. Again the destination boxes have disappeared, and the picture must pre-date the end of 1921 when all the female tram staff were summarily dismissed by the council.

14.   This view of the west end of Chatsworth Road shows the central line taken by the single track, and the twin pole and span wire construction which prevailed on the Brampton section of the system. Storrs Road is just off to the left, and a distant tram waits on the Vincent Crescent turnout.

15.   Car 11 approaches the same loop on a snowy winter's day, with one hardy soul sitting in splendid isolation on the freezing top deck. The track has been well swept, and on the right of the tram are open fields, now long since built over.

16. Taken from the open top of a car from the opposite direction to 15, the loop can just be seen at the foot of the photograph. The right hand tram pole carries a white band, indicating a stopping place until the advent of metal signs in 1919. Note the row of new houses being built at the top left.

17. Lower down the road a group of children pose for the camera, which shows good detail of the track and running wire at this point. I doubt if they would be so foolhardy as to stand in the same place today! The trees on the left flank the grounds of St Thomas's Church.

18.   Looking west with the church on the right, this shot exemplifies the short-term difficulties caused by tracklaying during the late summer of 1904. Piled spoil fills the left side of the road, leaving only a narrow ribbon on the right, neatly blocked by the parked cart.

19. One of the 'Old and New Car' theme shots, this example poses Horse Car 8, driver Ezra Coates, with spanking new Electric Tram 7, pictured on the St Thomas's loop. The figure on the left of the equestrian is Chief Inspector Frank Root, horse tram inspector, newly promoted to run the new fleet. Amazingly, this view was recreated at Crich in the summer of 1997, though No.7 appeared there in top-covered guise.

20. Eades Horse Car 2 is here shown at Walton Lane (later Road), which was the western terminus for the horse trams. Note the youthful conductor, and the termination of the twin tracks behind the rear hoofs of the horses. This spot is now a busy roundabout.

21. Again taken from the open top of a tramcar, this view looks eastward along a sunny Chatsworth Road just beyond the junction with Walton Road. The overhead lines, passing above the cameraman's head, were raised 21ft 6in/6.5metres above road level. Many of the buildings seen here still stand, and on the far right is the entrance to Walton Fields Road.

22.   The previous photograph was taken in the left distance. In this shot Chatsworth Road meets Old Road on the right, the site of a passing loop whose rails can be seen in the road surface at the bottom left. Above can be seen the layout of the running wire, spaced out to allow for the turnout. The central building was the Police Station, now swept away to allow for a roundabout. The junction was a dangerous place for road traffic, especially in foggy weather.

→

23.   Chatsworth Road was occasionally inundated during heavy storms as in this view taken on 7th August 1922 when the River Hipper overflowed. Here one of the balcony cars is stranded below Barker Lane, with the Congregational Church on the left, as rising waters bring the system to a standstill.

→

24.   On the first test run along the Brampton section of the line, on 3rd December 1904, Horse Car 7 greets its replacement, Electric Car 9 in watery sunshine just outside the new tramshed. The muddy state of the thoroughfare is very apparent.

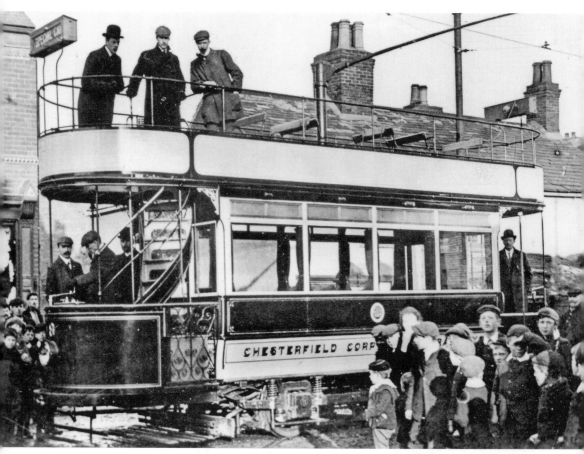

25. Car 9 is at rest by School Board Lane, the interested spectators being largely represented by pupils from the nearby school. The immaculate condition of the tramcar, not yet cluttered with advertisements, shows up well. Robert Acland fiddles with the controls, whilst the car is largely manned with Brush Company staff.

TRAM DEPOT

26.   The Chatsworth Road tramshed, erected by Tramways department staff, was built of brick with a slate roof. The original edifice measured 126 by 46ft/38.4metres by 14metres and held 16 cars in four tracks set over inspection pits. It was enlarged in 1914 to cater for cars 16-18. Note the tower wagon on the left of the shed.

27.   The building still stands after a varied career as a store shed for the East Midlands Electricity Board when the tram depot closed in 1927. It now houses a fleet, not of tramcars, but ice cream vans. The 1914 extension can be clearly seen on the far side of the building.

28. The complicated trackwork of the 'Y' layout at the entrance to the tramshed shows up well in this official photograph taken by British Helsby, the company who constructed the tramway. This work was in progress by mid-October, and the usual sightseers have materialized to hamper the workforce.

30. An excellent study of the tramshed turnout, with the 'Y' junction just visible in the distance. Chatsworth Road traffic must have remained at a complete standstill during this phase of construction.

29. Another shot taken at the junction shows both sets of curving rails joining the turnout situated on the main road. An officer of the law oversees arrangements, and yet another baby-in-arms is paraded for the camera.

31.   Great excitement must have accompanied the arrival of the first electric trams, loaded onto flat cars at the nearby Factory Street siding of the Midland Railway. Here the struck-down body of tram 10 arrives at the depot. Again a police constable keeps a watching brief on events. The overhead is still being strung; note the cable drum on the left, which contained some half-mile of hard-drawn copper wire.

32.   Car 7, pulled by a team of straining horses, rolls onto Chatsworth Road by the Barrel Inn which can be seen behind the front platform of the conveyance. The track has been laid though the filthy state of the road makes this hard to believe! The large dog sitting on the left views the event with some interest.

33.   Another 'Old and New Car' shot lines up Horse Car 8 in front of struck-down Electric Car 7 in front of the 'Public Refreshment Room' opposite the entrance to the tramshed.

34.   At rest in the depot yard, Car 7 awaits unloading and the fitting of its component parts. The photograph shows clearly the already-applied livery, and the Brush Company advertising bill in the tram window.

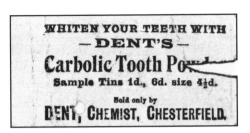

35.   A superb study features the newly delivered cars in the tramshed. Car 9, which took part in the first trials, is fully assembled apart from the upper deck wire mesh. Car 6 sports the netting, but has no lifeguards, whilst Cars 7 and 8 are still in the process of construction. A line of trolley masts can be seen along the wall to the left.

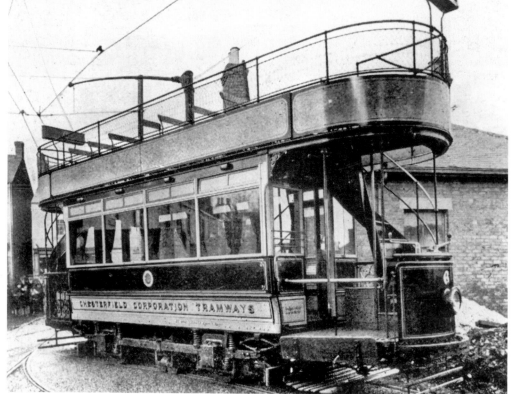

36.   The entrance to the tram depot has the office block fronting Chatsworth Road, with the tramshed behind. Note the dash panel propped against the wall inside the gates, and the 'Y' junction leading out onto the main thoroughfare.

37.   Newly-completed Car 6, patent brass bar at the horizontal, stands in its pristine glory in the depot yard, with an admiring crowd in view behind. To the right can be seen the rear of the tramway offices.

38.   One of the 13-14 class tramcars, illuminated for the 1910 September Shopping festival, is shown lit up in the yard, with the crew alongside. The Electrical Energy Department provided the fixtures and bulbs at a cost of £25.

40. The tramshed is seen after the right-hand extension added in 1914. In this wartime shot Balcony Car 17 is seen undergoing complete refurbishment, probably after the October 1916 depot fire when the conveyance was totally gutted. Note the pile of controllers stacked on the right.

39. An excellent frontal view has Balcony Car 18 as new, standing on the tramshed loop sometime in the Summer of 1914 with the 'Y' junction rails in front of and behind the tram. The motorman is Horace Hall who appears as a youthful twelve-something in plate 62. On his right is Harry Longden, a veteran horse and electric car stalwart who later drove the very last tram when the service closed.

A – 8454

CHESTERFIELD
CORPORATION TRAMWAY

EXCHANGE
TICKET

Up

Brampton

Walton
Road

Market

Dark
Lane

Whitt-
ington

DOWN

Bell Punch Company, London

41.   The August 1922 floods also submerged Chatsworth Road outside the tram depot. Here another of the top-covered cars is stranded immediately outside the shed, watched by a considerable crowd apparently oblivious to the rain.

CHATSWORTH ROAD EAST

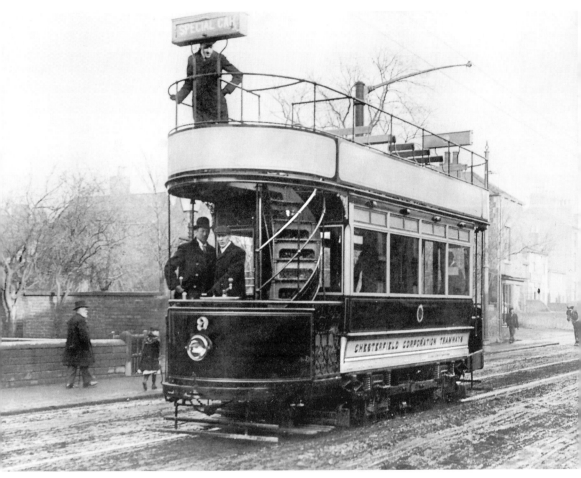

42.   Car 9 on its inaugural test pauses for its photograph somewhere near the entrance to Hipper Street, though the old gentleman on the left seems completely unaware of the example of progress passing by.

43. In much the same vicinity is Car 7 on an outing on December 6th 1904. On the platform, in his new uniform, is Chief Inspector Frank Root, who served in this office for over 20 years, after a stint as inspector of the horse tramway.

──────────►

44. Eade's two-decker Car 1 plods stoically up Chatsworth Road at a steady two miles an hour, sometime around 1900. On the left is the entrance to Brook Yard, with the Mason's Arms on the far right. This locality is still recognizable over 100 years later.

──────────►

45. From the opposite direction Nadin's camera picks out Car 1 standing on the gasworks loop with the Mason's Arms on the right. On the left hand side of the road was the premises of the Brampton Brewery, now replaced by a hideous looking B&Q store. The usual bystanders add animation to the scene.

WEST BARS

46.   One of the oldest photographs in the book may be this view of one of the Eade's double-deckers standing outside the Square and Compass public house on West Bars. A juvenile conductor manages to obscure the fleet number, and the style of lining-out on the rocker panel suggests a pre-1897 date before the corporation takeover. The advertising boards are as yet unsullied.

47.   Single-deck Horse Car 8 is seen on a muddy West Bars with Clarence Road visible on the far right. This photograph, probably taken during the last winter of service, reveals the salient features of these little trams. The driver is Ezra Coates, horse and conductor unknown.

48.   In a leafy West Bars, the entrance to West House, once the home of Lady Baden Powell, is glimpsed on the right. Horse Car 8 passes an unidentified single-decker on the loop, whilst the carts show that horse transport was still the main mode of road travel.

49. Some 20 years later in the same area, the little water car, No.15, heads off the turnout towards town, spraying everything in sight using its 2000 gallon/9092litres tank. The vehicle could hose down a 50ft/15metres wide area, but after the Great War was little used. This view, showing the tram in operation, with the Market Place railway station on the right, is unique.

50. A picture of the service car on the Brush Company traverser, without electrics, but with a snowplough fixed to the right-hand end. Boasting a Brush long wheelbase truck measuring 8ft 6in, the car cost £744 when purchased in 1909. A similar vehicle was later provided for the York system.

51. At the eastern end of West Bars, near the Stanton Brothers premises, one of the 13-14 class trams shows off its plumage for the 1910 eight-day Shopping Festival and is conveniently posed in front of Nadin, the photographer's, premises. Behind the conveyance is an ordinary service tram.

NEW SQUARE

52.   Near the end of its journey into town, one of the Eade's two-deckers halts by the Sun Inn on the left, and the new Portland Hotel on the right. Note the knifeboard seating arrangement on the upper deck of the tram. The crowds suggest a busy market day Saturday.

53.   Compare this view with the last as Electric Car 6 heads for Brampton, despite the 'MARKET PLACE' destination on its indicator box. The Sun Inn has not yet suffered its makeover in 'Public Convenience' style, with white, cream and brown glazed tiling. Again, the distant stalls imply a Saturday date.

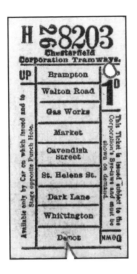

54.   Car 14, new in 1907, heads for the Low Pavement halt in another busy study of New Square by Dent's Chemist's Corner. Note the rail junction behind the tram, with the left-hand rails curving up into the town centre. On Saturdays the cars were barred from the central streets of Chesterfield, due to crowd congestion.

55.   An excellent shot shows Car 4 heading up New Square onto the double line which ran through the centre of the township, some time during the first winter of service. The conductor eyes the camera, whilst the top-deck passenger holds on as the conveyance swings round the curve. On the right is the Market Hall, below which a pile of stone setts show that road paving is still in progress. The conservatory-style shed, topped by a stove chimney, sheltered the horse cab drivers whose hackney stand was nearby.

56. Looking down from the opposite direction, this World War 1 shot shows why the through-town route was closed on Saturdays. The twin track can be seen on both sides of the bicycle, whilst a balcony car can just be seen nosing into view by the Dent's sign on the right.

57. In this 1923 photograph, Balcony Car 16 pauses on its way to Brampton by the Portland Hotel in an almost deserted New Square. In the foreground the tram rails can be seen opening out into double track, amidst a sea of cobblestones. Soon after this view was taken the Low Pavement spur was abandoned for the construction of underground toilets.

LOW PAVEMENT

58. Car 1 proceeds gingerly along the Low Pavement single line amidst the market day stalls and crowds. Take away the tramlines and overhead, and the view is much the same to this day.

→

59. In this 1890s scene, Horse Car 5, still run by the Chesterfield Tramway Company, waits at the town terminus, giving clear detail of its design and livery. Note the square-headed windows, the lack of clerestory windows in the roof, and the casual gear of the crew. Eyre's furnishers had the sole advertising rights on trams and tickets at this time.

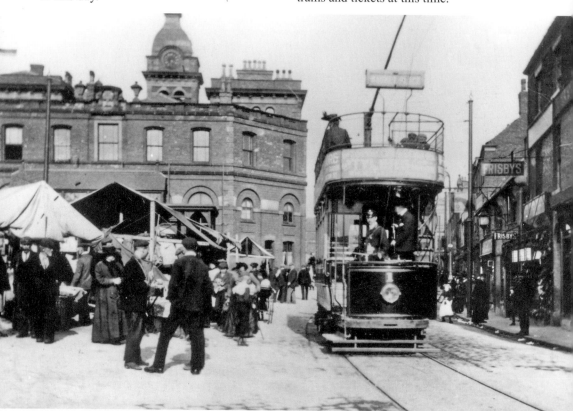

→

60. Car 8 is seen again, with Ezra Coates controlling a pair of horses at the same venue, halted by a fairly laden young conductor. Compare the features of this tram with Car 5 seen in the previous picture, and note the busy display in Tyler's shoe shop window opposite.

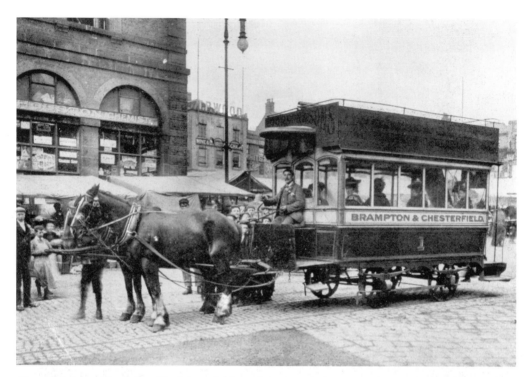

61.   Eade's double-decker No.1 is at the Low Pavement halt, surrounded by an interested cluster of youngsters. Details of the patent truck and the stone paving holding the tramlines show up well. Though the lower saloon is well patronised, the upper deck remains as yet empty.

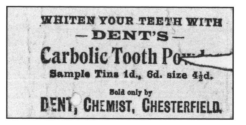

62.   Single-deck Horse Car 7 is at the same venue, as a passenger climbs aboard at the rear of the two-horse conveyance. In the distance can be seen the premises of T.P. Wood, wine and spirit merchants, Whites music shop and Hadfield's pork butchers. The driver is Seth Hall, the conductor his son Horace, who appears as a motorman in picture 39.

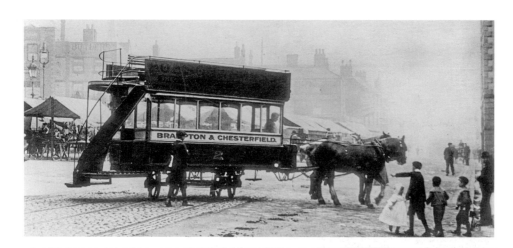

63.   This is a fine shot of Eade's Car 2 at the end of the track terminations at the bottom end of the Market Place. The vehicle is being turned by the side-stepping horses who are swivelling the car body around the axis of the rigid truck for the journey to Brampton. This type of patent truck allowed for a lighter conveyance by obviating the need for two staircases.

64.   Tracklaying is seen at the upper end of New Square in the autumn of 1904. The double rails are being positioned outside the Market Hall Coffee Rooms. The white board below the sign lists the good things on the café menu.

65.   A superb shot shows three electric cars, Nos. 9, 8 and 11, running along the twin track neatly laid in its bed of limestone setts. The Post Office still stands on the left of the scene today, and on the right rival forms of transport take time off for a feed. Though Car 9 is heading for Whittington, the conductor has failed to reset the destination box.

66.   This commercial postcard shows the view looking along the top of the Market Place towards High Street, and includes the layout of the running wire at this point. The thoroughfare is very wide at this point, though it narrows considerably towards High Street in the distance.

67.   An excellent vista of the top end of the Market Place, as lightly loaded Car 1 halts to allow boarders to embark for Brampton. The double line can be clearly seen here as it heads right towards High Street and the heart of the township. The archways, now sadly gone, mark the premises of T.P. Wood, wine and spirit merchant, and long-serving councillor, alderman and mayor of the borough.

HIGH STREET

68.   T.P. Wood's archways are on the left in this scene which looks along High Street in October 1904 as tracklaying virtually brought the town centre to a standstill for six weeks, to the chagrin of the local shopkeepers. Though the line is being positioned, the bracket-arm traction poles still lack their bowstring supports and running wire. The usual idlers gather on the pavement to watch less fortunate mortals toil!

69. Further east where High Street becomes Burlington Street, the tracklaying continues apace, as the shops attempt to recoup their losses by an autumn sale. Note how narrow the road width is for double track, and the strategically placed planks to allow the braver pedestrians to cross the rails.

BURLINGTON STREET

70.   A good view taken along Burlington Street looking west as the lines push through the town centre. The photograph gives an excellent sighting of the variety of Edwardian shop frontages along the thoroughfare. By this time the finely scrolled traction posts have received their bowstrings, but not as yet the overhead.

71.   Probably taken on the same day as plate 55, Car 4, driven by Motorman Stone, pauses on Burlington Street. Note the narrow space between the nearside of the tram and the pavement kerb. High on the right-hand wall can be seen the metal replica of an old type beehive, the trademark of the Beehive Drapery.

73.   Two cars slowly rumble past each other along the roadway, dwarfed by the Crooked Spire of St Mary and All Saint's Church. Behind the right-hand vehicle is the house of Dr Green, a local physician.

72.   An evocative study of Burlington Street in the twilight of the tramway era, taken just after 11.30am with a distant balcony car about to take the sharp curve into Stephenson Place. Note the beehive is now hung in front of Swallow's shop wall, one of three of these replicas originally visible along the street.

74. Tracklaying proceeds at the east end of Burlington Street, with the line beginning the 48ft/14.6metres radius curve into Stephenson Place, the severest bend on the line. Concrete has already been laid between the rails and the usual urchins pose on the cross-street planks.

75. At the corner the sharp curve of the track at this point can be appreciated. A fine decorated bracket-arm pole can be seen on the left, and one can sympathise with Dr Green, as service cars clattered past the front door of his residence from an early hour. The building was later demolished to make a way through to the parish church.

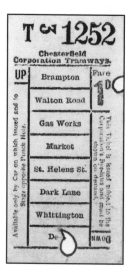

T 2 1252

Chesterfield
Corporation Tramways.

UP		Fare
	Brampton	1D
	Walton Road	
	Gas Works	
	Market	
	St. Helens St.	
	Dark Lane	
	Whittington	
	De	NWOD

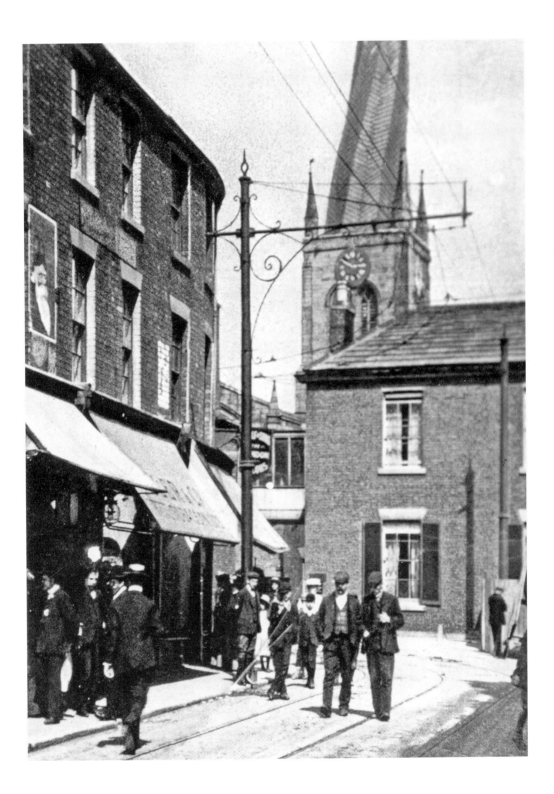

76.   This view may puzzle modern Cestrefeldians, but Dr Green's residence stands just to the right of Car 4 as it approaches the facing crossover at the entrance to Cavendish Street, having just negotiated the Burlington Street curve. Knifesmithgate, shown by the street sign high on the left-hand wall, was at this time much longer, before the eastern end was renamed Stephenson Place in the 1920s to commemorate the great railway engineer who died at Tapton House in 1848.

77.   Tracklaying around the curve in late October 1904 reveals the through-town chaos at this time, which led to much acrimonious discussion in council and the local press. A venturesome lady 'crosses the plank' in this busy scene. The shop frontages in the distance have completely changed over the last hundred years.

CAVENDISH STREET

78.   We look down Cavendish Street as labourers apply the finishing touches to the facing crossover which allowed cars to stand side-by-side at the weekend terminus. City House on the right was soon to be swept away for a new bank.

79.   The same corner is seen in around 1910, with the imposing façade of Deacon's Bank replacing the former clothing stores. Note the sharpness of the curve as it swings left then right down Cavendish Street.

80.   The same scene near the end of the tramway era as Car 10, still an open-topper, awaits passengers for Whittington. The crossover can be clearly seen, and the backseat lady driver in the imposing automobile on the right is doubtless directing operations. The shop frontages on the left still survive intact.

81.   The last few weeks of tramway operation in town were in 1927. The conductor swings the trolleyboom of Car 7, now top-covered, for its journey to Whittington. By this time the Brampton route was being converted to trolleybus operation, and the aggressive-looking Bristol motorbus (RA 441) on the right was providing a temporary service before the trackless takeover.

82.   The inevitable loungers, mostly well dressed, display deep interest in the proceedings as the workmen put the finishing touches to the crossover in bright autumn sunshine.

83.   Lower down Cavendish Street at an earlier stage in the proceedings, labourers busily excavate the road under the gaze of bemused spectators. The disruption caused by the arrival of tramways in towns can be readily appreciated by this view.

84. Nadin's camera catches the tracklaying as it approaches Holywell Cross at the north end of Cavendish Street, a much run-down area at the time to judge by the buildings on the right.

85. An opposite view shows the same street under siege. By this time the roadway has been levelled and the twin track laid. A variety of goods, edible and otherwise, grace the windows of the shops, though I doubt modern health inspectors would have fancied the poultry on display!

86. Car 8 waits along the street in the summer of 1905, dated by sale notices on City House on the right, before its demolition that same year. Some neatly dressed youngsters pose for their pictures, below the three ornate gas lamps above the shop window. The ladies in shot display some notable headgear.

87. A superb tramscape of the street, with bracket poles carrying the running wire. The two cyclists make sure their wheels avoid the grooves in the tram rail. The only buildings now standing in this scene are those in the distance.

HOLYWELL CROSS

88.   Holywell Cross bears a distinctly down-market appearance in this scene, with derelict-looking buildings occupying the corner where Eyres shop now stands, with the old Bell public house on the opposite corner. The tramlines here are laid in tarmac, and a faded policeman directs traffic at this busy intersection in a view which dates to around 1910.

89.   Car 11 halts at the stop by Coopers confectioners, marked by the white band on the traction pole. The premises on the left are Damm's fruiterers, and in the distance another tram can just be discerned. The Primitive Methodist Church is still there, but now serves a different purpose.

HOLYWELL STREET

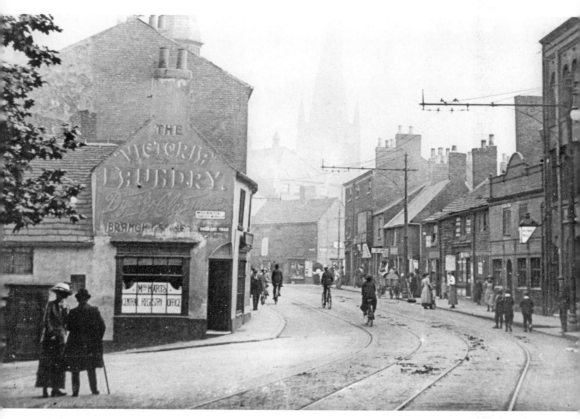

90.   Holywell Street looking towards town, with a ghostly Crooked Spire just visible on a misty day. The line is still twin-track, and the overhead is supported on 25ft/7.6metres high side-arm poles ornamented with wrought-iron scrolling. The line of buildings on the right have been swept away for a car park.

91.   A tree-lined Holywell Street during the last period of the trams, with the Royal Hospital grounds on the left, and the twin tracks encased in tarmac. An unidentified open-topper lurks in the shade on the right, and the bracket poles have been shorn of their scrollwork.

92.   The sharp bend of the double track at the junction of Newbold Road (left) and Sheffield Road occurs just before the line becomes single again in this much-changed scene which is now dominated by a roundabout. Distant adverts extol the programmes at the Hippodrome and Corporation Theatres. Note the stove-enamelled stop sign on the bracket pole, which must boast one of the longest bracket-arms on the system.

←

93.   A wintry scene just round the right-hand corner from the previous view as the through-town rails were linked with the Sheffield Road ones by Holywell House, seen on the left. A policeman regulates the chaos, as the blocked roadway obviously necessitated a detour to Whittington via Newbold Road on the left.

95.   A well-laden Car 2 tackles the incline above the Holy Trinity loop around 1910 in this Nadin view, which can be contrasted with the previous photograph, and shows the fine replacement wall in a landscape now much shorn of its trees.

←

94.   A first-rate view of the earlier tracklaying in August 1904 as the British Helsby workforce construct the Holy Trinity Church loop just below Holywell House. Note the stone setts on the right, ready for laying, and the motley group of navies and spectators. The crumbling wall on the left was soon to be rebuilt as the frontage to the new girls' grammar school.

96.   Workmen busily clean the points as Car 6 lingers on the next turnout to the north by St Helen's Street outside Day's drapery as passengers embark for town. The tin shack alongside is a nonconformist chapel which my mother used to clean during World War 2.

97.   Nadin again uses the upper deck of a tram as it pauses on the next loop by Albert Street, with the line well to the side of the road to cater for the bracket poles. On 8th October 1926, Car 8 jumped the rails at this loop and wedged itself between the post on the right and a butcher's shop. At the bottom left is the entrance to Hardwick Street, home of the future transport department, opened in 1927.

98.   The very accident, as Car 8 pays an unscheduled visit to Watson's butchers around 7pm on the day in question. Mercifully the tram standard prevented the vehicle from toppling, and injuries were few. Points to notice include the stop sign on the pole, the simplified black lettering on the rocker panel, and the destination boards in the saloon windows of the tram. The vehicle was back in service by early December.

99. The narrow road is by the derelict Jug and Glass pub on the left. A shot taken in March 1922, is nicely dated by the adverts proclaiming 'The Mark of Zorro' with Douglas Fairbanks, playing at the Corporation Theatre that month. Car 1, still open-topped, waits by the stop sign. In June 1906, Car 6 demolished an inoffensive coal-cart at this spot.

——————→

100. The same scene is repeated after road widening, with the pub now replaced by a smart new house and with twin poles and span wire taking over from the old bracket arms. The side road on the left is Stonegravels Lane, now the entrance to the cleansing department.

——————→

101. Looking northwards from the same area, the other side of the stop sign can be clearly seen on the right, and on the left is the brand-new frontage to the much improved road. The twin-track ran from this locality to Dark Lane in the far distance.

DARK lANE

←————

102. A very rare study: Car 11 heads for Whittington, in a photograph which can only have been taken between January and May 1905, when the single line was replaced by twin-track in order to cut out problems caused by the right-hand blind bend in the distance by Dark Lane, which hid oncoming trams.

←————

103. Manager Robert Acland is able to obscure the fleet number of the waiting tram, as he supervises the doubling of the track, with Dark Lane off to the right. It seems incredible that parts of the system were once so rural, especially as this peaceful locality is now covered by a noisy roundabout. Acland is standing on the original single line.

104. Not the finest of prints, but it shows an interesting tramscape at the Whittington end of Sheffield Road, with Car 10 heading for town under a line of bracket poles, with the local school behind the wall on the right. The first ever accident on the tramway occurred here on a wet March night in 1905 when a tramcar rammed two horse-drawn railway drays, though without serious injury to either men or beasts.

105. Further up the slope, the line moves to the roadside, as Car 7 in the distance, leaves the Whittington terminus for town. The scene remains much the same today, though without the horse-drawn vehicles! Note how the telegraph lines on the left have forced the use of side-arm poles to carry the running wire on the right.

106. Heading for the terminus, the single track shows up well in its bed of stone setts in this animated vista, as groups of children, evidently in their Sunday best, pose for Nadin's lens. Foundry Street is just off to the right, with the Brunswick Hotel on the corner.

Chesterfield Corporation Tramways

FARES

TO OR FROM

Brampton and Gas Works	1d.
Walton Road and Stephenson Place	1d.
Gas Works and Albert Street	1d.
Stephenson Place and Dark Lane	1d.
Albert Street and Whittington	1d.
Brampton and Stephenson Place	1½d.
Brampton and Market Place	1½d.
Stephenson Place and Whittington	1½d.
Gas Works and Dark Lane	1½d.
Walton Road and Dark Lane	2d.
Brampton and Albert Street	2½d.
Gas Works and Whittington	2½d.
Through	3d.

WORKMEN'S CARS

Before 8 a.m. from Brampton or Whittington and 8-10 a.m. from Market Place.

Brampton and Stephenson Place	1d.
Stephenson Place and Whittington	1d.
Walton Road and Albert Street	1d.

Children over 3 Years of Age must be paid for.

Children under the age of 10 are allowed to travel for a 1d. over a 1½d. Section.

No fares or excess fares less than One Penny will be accepted.

No Through Tickets between Brampton and Whittington will be issued unless a Through Service is run.

No change can be given by the Conductor for a coin of larger value than Half-a-Crown.

PASSENGERS ARE RESPECTFULLY REQUESTED TO OBSERVE THAT THE CONDUCTOR PUNCHES A TICKET REPRESENTING THE VALUE OF THE FARE PAID FOR AND THE SECTION TO BE TRAVELLED OVER.

PASSENGERS MUST NOT GET ON OR LEAVE THE CAR WHILE IN MOTION.

TRAMWAY DEPOT,
172, CHATSWORTH ROAD,
APRIL, 1919.

R. L. ACLAND, M.Inst.E.E.,
Engineer.

WHITTINGTON TERMINUS

107. A service car waits at the terminus in the distance, behind a specially hired tramcar, employed to take refreshments to the other end of the line for some 2,000 children for their annual picnic at Somersall. James Thompson, a local baker, held the contract, and he can be seen on the car platform in this 1913 study. Thompson's Belsize van stands alongside the tram, which is towing a water boiler running on an old horse-car truck. Note the 'TRAILER BEHIND' sign on the dash, with 'SPECIAL CAR' on the destination blind.

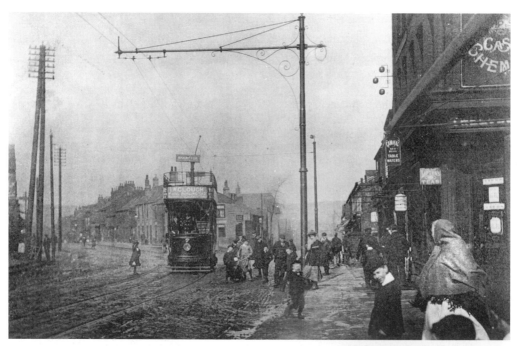

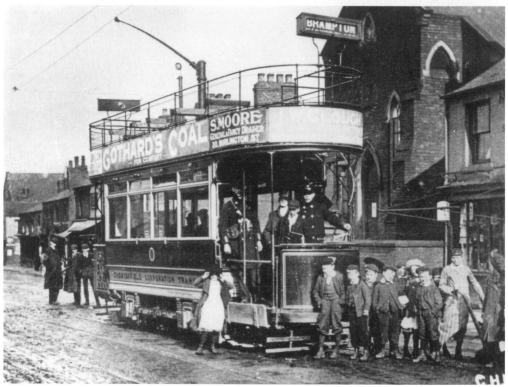

108. Car 7 noses into the terminus on a filthy stretch of road, with the Black Horse pub behind. Sheffield Road veers off to the left, and the fine scrolled bracket standard on the right was soon to be replaced by twin poles and span wire.

109. Car 7 is at the terminus in a picture taken shortly after the previous one. Note the horizontal bar and folded platform step, and the group of urchins placed in shot for the postcard which was probably on sale within hours of being taken!

110. Originally the tramway was intended to run some 500 yards further along Sheffield Road on the left, terminating at the New Inn and its junction with Brimington Road. In the event the line stopped just below Duke Street on the Whittington UDC boundary, and, despite promises, never penetrated beyond this point.

111. This is where the tramway should have continued, but failed to do so. In the distance can be seen the actual terminus, with a service car just visible behind the pony and trap to the right of the steamroller. The local council feared lost revenue from this curtailment of the line, as it could have carried local colliers to the pit at Sheepbridge.

112. A frontal shot of Car 9 at Whittington has building work visible on the right. The kepi-style caps of the crew place the picture in the early years of the service. Note the clumsy and oversized destination boxes, which were not abandoned until after the First World War.

113. A less than perfect photograph, but it captures the terminal double track at Whittington, which allowed two trams to park side-by-side in what looks like a snowy winter scene.

114. Taken from the opposite direction, this shot picks out the track terminations as they curve along Sheffield Road, with a departing car 'hull down' on the horizon. One of my relatives, a conductor in 1926, once failed to set the handbrake on the rear platform, with the result that his tram ran back off the end of the track here and sank into the soft tarmac! A lorry had to drag the conveyance back onto the line.

115. Car 11 is at Whittington with everyone in sight attempting to get in shot. Note how the earlier bracket pole has been replaced with twin poles and supporting span wire. Presumably the earlier arrangement did not give sufficient clearance for the trolleybooms, when two cars were parked alongside each other.

116. A World War 1 shot has Car 9 outside
Shentall's grocers, an appropriate venue, as
Ernest Shentall was chairman of the Tramways
Committee at the time. Opposite, a fine Shire
horse stands outside Hunter's Ltd., which
displays an interesting array of contemporary
goods and prices. Queen Street appears on the
right in this photograph.

117. A much retouched postcard shows Balcony
Car 18 at the terminus sometime after the end of
the war. Note how the camera has failed to pick
up the vehicle's trolleyboom, whilst the overhead
wire has disappeared completely!

END OF AN ERA

118. Car 14 featured in the final run to Whittington on a damp 23rd May 1927, suitably bedecked with flags and bunting, though dilapidated and dented. The motorman was stalwart Harry Longden, then night depot foreman, whilst the passengers included civic dignitaries, councillors and other guests.

119. The tram bowed out at the Chatsworth Road tramshed later the same day, as brand-new Straker-Clough trolleybus No.1 waited to freight the prominenti on its first service run. On the far right is Tramways Committee Chairman Philip Robinson, with Mayor Harry Cropper on his right. Fourth in line is Manager Walter Marks.

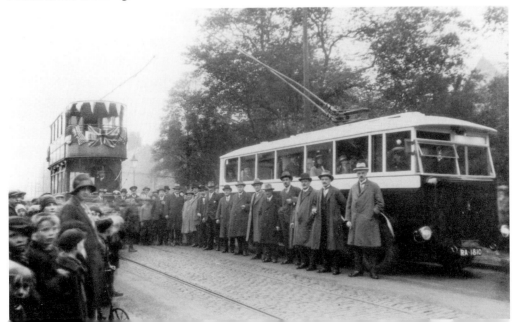

FINALE

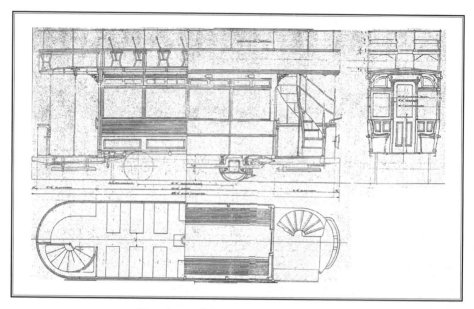

Drawings of Cars 1-14 at 4mm to 1ft.

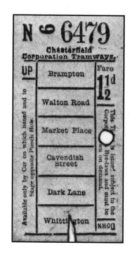

120. In the 1990s Crich Tramway Museum totally restored Car 7 which had fortunately been preserved as a holiday home at Two Dales, Derbyshire. Superbly renovated, the tram now runs regularly at the museum. Here, on 11th October 1999, the author takes a driving lesson along the line.

MP Middleton Press

Easebourne Lane, Midhurst, W Sussex. GU29 9AZ Tel: 01730 813169 Fax: 01730 812601
Email: sales@middletonpress.co.uk www.middletonpress.co.uk

If books are not available from your local transport stockist, order direct post free UK.

BRANCH LINES
Branch Line to Allhallows
Branch Line to Alton
Branch Lines around Ascot
Branch Line to Ashburton
Branch Lines around Bodmin
Branch Line to the Bude
Branch Lines around Canterbury
Branch Lines around Chard & Yeovil
Branch Line to Cheddar
Branch Lines around Cromer
Branch Line to the Derwent Valley
Branch Lines to East Grinstead
Branch Lines of East London
Branch Lines to Effingham Junction
Branch Lines to Enfield Town & Palace Gates
Branch Lines to Falmouth, Helston & St. Ives
Branch Line to Fairford
Branch Lines to Felixstow & Aldeburgh
Branch Lines around Gosport
Branch Line to Hayling
Branch Lines to Henley, Windsor & Marlow
Branch Line to Hawkhurst
Branch Line to Horsham
Branch Lines around Huntingdon
Branch Line to Ilfracombe
Branch Line to Kingsbridge
Branch Line to Kingswear
Branch Line to Lambourn
Branch Lines to Launceston & Princetown
Branch Lines to Longmoor
Branch Line to Looe
Branch Line to Lyme Regis
Branch Line to Lynton
Branch Lines around March
Branch Lines around Midhurst
Branch Line to Minehead
Branch Line to Moretonhampstead
Branch Lines to Newport (IOW)
Branch Lines to Newquay
Branch Lines around North Woolwich
Branch Line to Padstow
Branch Lines around Plymouth
Branch Lines to Princes Risborough
Branch Lines to Seaton and Sidmouth
Branch Lines around Sheerness
Branch Line to Shrewsbury
Branch Line to Tenterden
Branch Lines around Tiverton
Branch Lines to Torrington
Branch Lines to Tunbridge Wells
Branch Line to Upwell
Branch Line to Wantage (The Wantage Tramway)
Branch Lines of West London
Branch Lines of West Wiltshire
Branch Lines around Weymouth
Branch Lines around Wimborne
Branch Lines around Wisbech

NARROW GAUGE
Austrian Narrow Gauge
Branch Line to Lynton
Branch Lines around Portmadoc 1923-46
Branch Lines around Porthmadog 1954-94
Branch Line to Southwold
Douglas to Port Erin
Douglas to Peel
Kent Narrow Gauge
Northern France Narrow Gauge
Romneyrail
Sierra Leone Narrow Gauge
Southern France Narrow Gauge
Sussex Narrow Gauge
Surrey Narrow Gauge

Swiss Narrow Gauge
Two-Foot Gauge Survivors
Vivarais Narrow Gauge

SOUTH COAST RAILWAYS
Ashford to Dover
Bournemouth to Weymouth
Brighton to Eastbourne
Brighton to Worthing
Dover to Ramsgate
Eastbourne to Hastings
Hastings to Ashford
Ryde to Ventnor
Southampton to Bournemouth

SOUTHERN MAIN LINES
Basingstoke to Salisbury
Crawley to Littlehampton
Dartford to Sittingbourne
East Croydon to Three Bridges
Epsom to Horsham
Exeter to Barnstaple
Exeter to Tavistock
London Bridge to East Croydon
Tonbridge to Hastings
Salisbury to Yeovil
Sittingbourne to Ramsgate
Swanley to Ashford
Tavistock to Plymouth
Three Bridges to Brighton
Victoria to Bromley South
Victoria to East Croydon
Waterloo to Windsor
Waterloo to Woking
Woking to Portsmouth
Woking to Southampton
Yeovil to Exeter

EASTERN MAIN LINES
Barking to Southend
Ely to Kings Lynn
Ely to Norwich
Fenchurch Street to Barking
Hitchin to Peterborough
Ilford to Shenfield
Ipswich to Saxmundham
Liverpool Street to Ilford
Saxmundham to Yarmouth
Tilbury Loop

WESTERN MAIN LINES
Banbury to Birmingham
Bristol to Taunton
Didcot to Banbury
Didcot to Swindon
Ealing to Slough
Exeter to Newton Abbot
Moreton-in-Marsh to Worcester
Newton Abbot to Plymouth
Newbury to Westbury
Oxford to Moreton-in-Marsh
Paddington to Ealing
Paddington to Princes Risborough
Plymouth to St. Austell
Princes Risborough to Banbury
Reading to Didcot
Slough to Newbury
St. Austell to Penzance
Swindon to Bristol
Swindon to Newport
Taunton to Exeter
Westbury to Taunton

MIDLAND MAIN LINES
Bedford to Wellingborough
Euston to Harrow & Wealdstone
Gloucester to Bristol
Harrow to Watford
St. Albans to Bedford
St. Pancras to St. Albans

COUNTRY RAILWAY ROUTES
Abergavenny to Merthyr
Andover to Southampton
Bath to Evercreech Junction
Bath Green Park to Bristol
Bournemouth to Evercreech Junction
Brecon to Newport
Burnham to Evercreech Junction
Cheltenham to Andover
Croydon to East Grinstead
Didcot to Winchester
East Kent Light Railway
Fareham to Salisbury
Frome to Bristol
Guildford to Redhill
Reading to Basingstoke
Reading to Guildford
Redhill to Ashford
Salisbury to Westbury
Stratford upon Avon to Cheltenham
Strood to Paddock Wood
Taunton to Barnstaple
Wenford Bridge to Fowey
Westbury to Bath
Woking to Alton
Yeovil to Dorchester

GREAT RAILWAY ERAS
Ashford from Steam to Eurostar
Festiniog in the Fifties
Festiniog in the Sixties
Festiniog 50 years of enterprise
Isle of Wight Lines 50 years of change
Railways to Victory 1944-46
Return to Blaenau 1970-82
SECR Centenary album
Talyllyn 50 years of change
Wareham to Swanage 50 years of change
Yeovil 50 years of change

LONDON SUBURBAN RLYS
Caterham and Tattenham Corner
Charing Cross to Dartford
Clapham Jn. to Beckenham Jn.
Crystal Palace (HL) & Catford Loop
East London Line
Finsbury Park to Alexandra Palace
Holborn Viaduct to Lewisham
Kingston and Hounslow Loops
Lewisham to Dartford
Lines around Wimbledon
Liverpool Street to Chingford
Mitcham Junction Lines
North London Line
South London Line
West Croydon to Epsom
West London Line
Willesden Junction to Richmond
Wimbledon to Beckenham
Wimbledon to Epsom

STEAMING THROUGH
Steaming through Cornwall
Steaming through the Isle of Wight
Steaming through Kent
Steaming through West Hants

TRAMWAY CLASSICS
Aldgate & Stepney Tramways
Barnet & Finchley Tramways
Bath Tramways
Brighton's Tramways
Bristol's Tramways
Burton & Ashby Tramways
Camberwell & W.Norwood Tramways
Clapham & Streatham Tramways
Croydon's Tramways
Derby Tramways
Dover's Tramways
East Ham & West Ham Tramways
Edgware and Willesden Tramways
Eltham & Woolwich Tramways
Embankment & Waterloo Tramways
Exeter & Taunton Tramways
Fulwell – Home to Trams, Trolleys and Buses
Great Yarmouth Tramways
Greenwich & Dartford Tramways
Hammersmith & Hounslow Tramways
Hampstead & Highgate Tramways
Holborn & Finsbury Tramways
Ilford & Barking Tramways
Kingston & Wimbledon Tramways
Lewisham & Catford Tramways
Liverpool Tramways 1. Eastern Routes
Liverpool Tramways 2. Southern Routes
Liverpool Tramways 3. Northern Routes
Maidstone & Chatham Tramways
Margate to Ramsgate
North Kent Tramways
Norwich Tramways
Reading Tramways
Shepherds Bush & Uxbridge Tramways
Southend-on-sea Tramways
South London Line Tramways 1903-33
Southwark & Deptford Tramways
Stamford Hill Tramways
Twickenham & Kingston Tramways
Victoria & Lambeth Tramways
Waltham Cross & Edmonton Tramways
Walthamstow & Leyton Tramways
Wandsworth & Battersea Tramways

TROLLEYBUS CLASSICS
Bradford Trolleybuses
Croydon Trolleybuses
Darlington Trolleybuses
Derby Trolleybuses
Huddersfield Trolleybuses
Hull Trolleybuses
Portsmouth Trolleybuses
Reading Trolleybuses

WATERWAY & SHIPPING
Kent and East Sussex Waterways
London to Portsmouth Waterway
Sussex Shipping - Sail, Steam & Motor
West Sussex Waterways

MILITARY BOOKS
Battle over Portsmouth
Battle over Sussex 1940
Blitz over Sussex 1941-42
Bombers over Sussex 1943-45
Bognor at War
East Ridings Secret Resistance
Military Defence of West Sussex
Military Signals from the South Coast
Secret Sussex Resistance
Sussex Home Guard
Surrey Home Guard

OTHER RAILWAY BOOKS
Collectors for Trains, Trolleys & Trams
Industrial Railways of the South-East
South Eastern & Chatham Railways
London Chatham & Dover Railway
London Termini - Past and Proposed
War on the Line (SR 1939-45)

96